Last Dance of a Dalesman

A community play
for Richmondshire

by Nobby Dimon

\

Licence to perform this script may be obtained by
application to the author
via office@northcountrytheatre.com

Printed in the UK by Blissetts, London

ISBN 978-0-9574415-3-8

Published in 2020
Caroline Brannigan, Richmond, North Yorkshire
www.carolinebrannigan.com

What is a Community Play?

Any piece of drama which involves members of a particular community in working together could qualify for the title and in America the words Community Theatre usually refer to what we call amateur dramatics and operatics. The idea of the community play as it is best known in Britain stems largely from the work of playwright and director Anne Jellicoe and the Colway Theatre Trust in Dorset in the late 1970s. Her original formula was to commission an established professional writer to research and create a large scale new work about or relating in some way to the history and life of the local people. She combined professional actors and production team with a very large cast of volunteers and often staged these productions "promenade" with audience and actors mingling together.

I was lucky enough to take a party of school pupils to see her Lyme Regis community play "The Reckoning " in 1978 and it remains in my memory as one of the best theatrical experiences I have ever had. By a strange coincidence one of the professional actors working with her on that play was Martin Dower from the Medium Fair Theatre who, 27 years later, appeared in Last Dance as Dan Ottershaw.

The Richmondshire play project added three extra challenges to the usual formula. Firstly, we were going to perform outside. Secondly, we were going to perform in several venues (which to my knowledge had not been done with such a large cast before). Thirdly and perhaps most difficult, there is no "community" of Richmondshire as such, only a huge area of scattered settlements over several dales and three major towns (four including Catterick Garrison) with different histories and traditions and as much rivalry in those histories as co-operation.

We tried, however, to pull this "community" together and it's worth noting that the original cast included people from Hawes, Leyburn, Richmond, Catterick, Reeth and Gunnerside as well as many villages across the district. Though the play is mostly set in Swaledale it draws on stories and legends from across the district. You can't invent a "community" by staging a play but all drama is about a shared experience, our common humanity, and a sense of continuity with the people of the past and the people of the future. This play and project tried in a small way to make us feel the ties that bind us together rather than the things which pull us apart.

The main action of the play takes place in Swaledale in 1953, though the final scene is in the present (2005 when the play was first written and produced). Although real places and local sounding character names are used, the stories and characters are not based on any particular people or families and any resemblances are entirely coincidental.

That said, we did draw on a number of local traditions, legends and myths and especially the books, drawings and experiences of the late Marie Hartley. In 2005 Marie was a 99-year-old resident of Askrigg.

The Australian Connection

The play makes reference to the Australian Aboriginal idea of "dreaming" and "dreamtime". In 2005 Australian actor and director Verity Higgins was working with North Country Theatre and living in Richmond with her two youngest children. It seemed an interesting idea to create an Australian connection for the play as the 1950s was a time of high emigration to Australia and Canada. The final scene in which Kit Harker's Australian descendants return to his native land was thus originally performed by an Australian family.

Nobby Dimon

The Corpse Way

There is an ancient path, still used by walkers, passing down Swaledale from Keld to Grinton, which has become known as the Corpse Way. Before 1580, when a new burial ground was consecrated at Muker, the path was used by funeral parties carrying their dead down from the upper dale to the only consecrated ground at Grinton Church for burial. This sixteen mile journey would take two days and the pallbearers would leave the coffin overnight near Blades in the 'Dead House' then slip down to the Punch Bowl Inn for refreshments.

Pete Roe

Last Dance of a Dalesman was first produced in the summer of 2005 by North Country Theatre in association with Arts in Richmondshire and performed over nine nights in five venues around North Yorkshire: Middleham Castle, Hardraw Scar, Richmond Castle, Forcett Hall and Kiplin Hall. It was directed by Nobby Dimon.

Original Cast

Chorus

Ruth	Hazel Waldman
Eileen	Amanda Heitler
Eileen's daughters	Emily Clark
	Emma Towning
	Sarah Cresswell/Claire Smith
May	Mavis Palfreman
Margaret	Chloe Greenwood/Gill Hayes
Joan	Judith Brickwood/Anne Wilkie
Phyllis	Rhoda Fraser/Marcia Howard
Betty	Maureen Clayton/Pamela Moffat
Jane	Sue Tandy/Caroline Graham

The Harkers

Sarah	Beverley Limbrick*
Christopher (Kit)	Matthew Clark/Ben Lacey

Pallbearers

Frank Dobson (Funeral Director)	Nobby Dimon*
Bob	Bryn Roberts
Ian	Michael Waldman
Don	Kevan Fawkes
Bill	John Clarke/Robin Battersby*
Charlie	Howard Firth

The Mourners
Irene Ottershaw (Dan's widow)   Marjorie Solomon
Edna (Irene's sister)   Linda Baldry
Lucy (Irene's sister)   Hazel Smith
Jenny (Irene & Dan's daughter)   Dawn Clarkson
Arthur (Irene & Dan's son   Nathan Middlemass-Dry
Shirley Skellbrooke   Belinda Cunningham

Dream Characters
Dan Ottershaw (The dead man)   Martin Dower*
The Tollman   Alan Harpley
Dan's mother   Dawn Clarkson
Young Irene   Emily Clark
Young Edna   Sarah Cresswell/ Claire Smith
Young Lucy   Emma Towning
Young Jenny   Hermione Higgins
Young Arthur   Nicholas Heitler

Others
Mr and Mrs Hill-Walker   Jonathan Heitler
                                                           and Verity Higgins*
Vicar   Jonathan Heitler
Older Susan   Amanda Heitler

From Australia
Kate (Kit's daughter)   Verity Higgins*
Alex (Kate's daughter)   Hermione Higgins
Tom (Kate's son)   Emil Freund

The Simon Stone Sextet
Simon Stone   Dave Harris
Guitar/vocals   Steve Wade
Bass   Bryn Roberts
Clarinet   Alan Harpley
Trumpet   Emil Freund
Flute   Jonathan Heitler

Production team

Assistant Director	Verity Higgins
Music Director	Dave Harris
Set design and scenic art	Neil Palliser
Construction	Malcolm Wood
Costume	Barbara Blakeson
Marketing and fund-raising for North Country Theatre	Gillian Howells
Production admin for North Country Theatre	Jaqui Wood
Production assistant	Oskar Howells
For Arts in Richmondshire	Robin Battersby
	Janet Hall
	Christel Kibbat

denotes professional actor

Community plays are often written for the people who volunteer to be in them. In a reversal of the usual theatrical convention, the cast are there before the script and the writer's ideas are partly shaped by the number, gender, ages, talents and availability of those people. There was no audition process for the volunteer actors. Everyone who wanted to be in it was in it and the script created accordingly.

Musical Note

Particular music and songs are specified in the script. Producers are reminded that if they use music they should ensure they have the correct permissions.

Prologue

*Haunting Music suggestive of windswept land as **Chorus** and company bring out large umbrellas painted to appear like landscape, fields, walls, woods etc.*
*They arrange themselves into an image of the dales. The music cross fades into the sound of a live band. A funeral procession goes past led by the band (**The Simon Stone Sextet**). Pallbearers carrying a coffin, mourners, all obviously very tired. The band is playing Goodnight Irene. They disappear ...*
*A group of women (**the Chorus: Ruth, Eileen, her three girls, May, Margaret, Joan, Phyllis, Betty, Jane**) emerge*

Ruth   Here's where we should stand
                  To see the story
                  Up on Calver Hill

Eileen   *(Pointing)* Or on high Oxnop to command the scene
                  Both up and down these river-riven hills
                  From Ravenseat to Richmond and beyond

May   Or on Blea Barf, way up on Crackpot Moor

Margaret   Or Kisdon's higher still.

Joan   It's too obscured!

Phyllis   Well why not Addleborough's fortress cliffs?

1

Betty	Or flat topped Penhill crags That overlook broad bottomed Wensleydale From Hardraw Force to Harmby down the line
Jane	Yes. There's our vantage point Our bird's eye view of space and time
Eileen	Hold on From there you can't see Gunnerside or Grinton, Gilling West nor Kiplin Hall
Phyllis	No more than here gives sight of Semerwater, Middleham, or the Leyburn Shawl
Ruth	Let's agree on this No matter where we choose to gather No one point of view can see it all. For now, let this place stand for all the other Lead mines, meadows, sheep and dry-stone walls.
Eileen	And all the other stories great and small.
All	That's our role,
Ruth	To take this life And knit it up in narrative Till it makes some sense.
Eileen	To pull the threads together.
May	Tie loose ends.
Betty	To make folk feel a little better
All	When the dark descends.

MUSIC
Distant strains of Goodnight Irene

Ruth	Take Sarah Harker. (*She appears putting out folding tables, dusting*)
May	Runs a small hotel, halfway down a dale
Margaret	Lost her husband last year in Korea
Joan	Then the business starts to fail
Eileen	Got a son who doesn't half worry her
ALL	Trying hard, but all to no avail.

The Chorus and hills dissolve away

Scene 1

Outside a small Guest House

Sarah   Kit! Kit! - where are you! The tables not laid, a barrel to be brought up from the cellar. Kit! Fires to be laid and lit, beds to be made up. Christopher Harker – you lazy little tyke – have you done anything I asked you! Have you?! Anything? Not one single thing to help. Like father like son. Kit! If you don't come out from wherever you're hiding by the time I count ten I swear I'll ...

Kit   *(Emerging from inside a log box)* I'm here. I'm here.

Sarah   Oooo you little beggar! How long have you been in there? You must have heard me calling.

Kit   I think I fell asleep. I was dreaming ... I saw ...

Sarah   *(cutting him off)* They'll be here soon, the whole blooming party and nothing ready! What did I ask you to do this afternoon eh? What? It's not often I ask you to help and when I do you let me down. *(She pauses and changes tone)* It's hard for me an all, you know. You're not the only one that misses your dad, but we've a business to run here Kit, we have to make a living or sell up and move out of the Dale – life goes on. Come on, help me put up this trestle – we'll do tea out here if the weather holds up.

4

Kit	I wish we could. I wish we could leave here. I hate it here. Nothing ever happens except funerals. Stupid little village. Everybody knows everybody, everything old fashioned, like this stupid funeral! What's the point of it? I can't wait to get away.
Sarah	You don't mean that.
Kit	I do! Dad said we were going to leave this year. Immigrate to Australia.
Sarah	<u>Emi</u>grate. And don't start that again Christopher, I really can't be doing with it today. We've got Ottershaw's funeral party coming down off the tops in a couple of hours. It's the biggest booking we've had since your dad died. Please Christopher don't make it harder than it already is.
Kit	We don't know he is dead. Not for certain. He might still be a prisoner somewhere. Derek Outhwaite at school said there's prison camps hidden in the jungle and nobody knows for certain ...
Sarah	Kit stop it. Please. *(Pause)*
Kit	Is <u>he</u> coming?
Sarah	Who?
Kit	Mr Dobson.
Sarah	Of course he is. You know it's his job. I don't know what you've got against him. He's been very kind to me, to us, since your dad ...
Kit	He's not dead *(pause ... she hugs him)*
Sarah	Look I want you to make bit more effort. Where Mr Dobson's concerned. For my sake. Will you do that?

Kit	I suppose.
Sarah	Good. Now come on, buck up. Mrs Hargreaves is bringing her three daughters, so it won't be all old people. You like their Susan don't you?
Kit	*(mortified)* Mum!

ENTER CHORUS Sarah and Kit continue to work

Ruth	It's 1953 and living up a dale Or anywhere that's off the beaten track Can make a woman feel her isolation
Eileen	While working men are running with the pack, The housebound wife may find some consolation
May	In the sisterhood of neighbours, kin folk, friends.
Margaret	The church, the chapel or the W.I. make do and mend.
Ruth	Now Sarah – the cavalry's arrived. We are all here apart from Dotty. She's got a bit of trouble
	(Sarah looks questioningly)
All	Down below!
Sarah	Oh.
Ruth	Eileen's brought the funeral cakes. May's got the cheeses.
Sarah	Could you follow the old recipe I gave you Eileen?
Eileen	Oh aye. Caraway seeds everywhere in our kitchen. Mi Mother knew it, mind. They all used to do it at one time. I have had my girls on it all day haven't I girls?
3 Girls	Yes mum

6

Sarah	Here. There's aprons.

They all start to put them on, helping each other, chatting

Eileen	It's a funny old do this – are they really carrying him all the way down the Dale?
May	They set off from Keld first thing this morning.
Ruth	He asked for it in his will apparently. It's like they used to, way back.
Sarah	It all has to be just so. He left money to pay for it otherwise I don't think Irene would have bothered.
Margaret	Silly old fool.
May	Shush, don't speak ill of the dead – he weren't a bad old stick.
Joan	Still. Twelve stone in a coffin all the way to Grinton Church.
Phyllis	If you ask me he was always a miserable old sod. A burden to himself while he was alive and a burden to everybody else now he's gone.
May	He wasn't always like that. You didn't know him when he was young.
Phyllis	Well I know I've no right to an opinion, not being born round here.
Ruth	Phyllis you've lived here 30 years and you were only born in Northallerton.
May	Incomers.
Ruth	Come on let's set to. They'll be here before we know it.

Sarah	I am grateful, honestly. I'd have been stuck without you lot.
Eileen	That's what friends and neighbours are for. Isn't it girls?
Girls	Yes mum.
Margaret	Aye. There's got to be some compensation for living in the middle of nowhere.
Ruth	Now come on give us our orders, Mistress of the house.
Sarah	Well if you come into the Dining Room I've done up a little list of what needs doing.

They troop off chatting happily except 3 girls and Kit.

3 Girls	Hello Kit.
Susan	Are you coming to choir practice on Sunday?

He gets back in the log store. They look at other and Exit

Re-enter Phyllis, Betty and Jane laying the table, gossiping

Phyllis	You know how she got this booking don't you?
Betty	Goo on!
Phyllis	Well by rights it should have been a bigger place – the Punch Bowl or the Travellers. This little place can't cope.
Jane	It's a big do. They've hired a band.
Phyllis	Well anyway the Ottershaws left it to Wilberforce the Undertakers to sort everything.
Jane	... according to the old man's will - recreating the Old Corpse Way procession and that.

8

Betty	So?
Phyllis	Well who's head man at Wilberforce's?
Betty	Frank Dobson.
Jane	And who's been seen taking Sarah Harker to Market in Leyburn recently in his car?
Betty	Frank Dobson.
Phyllis	Exactly, and once to the pictures in Richmond I heard. "From Here to Eternity".
Betty	Ooh, Burt Lancaster in his swimming trunks and Frank Sinatra.
Jane	You don't have to be Einstein to put two and two together and make five.
Betty	So he fixed it for her to do the funeral tea and the stop-over. That'll be worth a bob or two.
Phyllis	No doubt she'll find a way to repay him.
Jane	Well fair enough I say, her husband's been dead and gone a year.
Phyllis	Missing presumed. Mind, if we're talking plain, he wasn't much use when he _was_ here.
Jane	Like that lad of hers.
Betty	I know.
Jane	Christopher.
Phyllis	Moping around, face like a wet weekend.

Jane	Thinks he's the only lad ever lost a father. There was plenty like him in the war.
Phyllis	He needs a man around.
Betty	Well Frank Dobson's not a bad man I suppose. A bit old for her though.
Jane	He's got a car. Could help her get this place back on its feet.
Phyllis	Bit creepy I think. I'd rather have Frank Sinatra –
All	Ooby dooby do *(laughing)*
Jane	This table's not very stable, is there owt we can wedge it up with?
Phyllis	Look in that log box.

Jane opens it to reveal Kit. He steps out, looking at them, rushes off.

Betty	Oo heck! Do you think he heard us?
Sarah *(off)*	Kit, Kit, what's a matter, come back here! *(entering)* What happened? *(awkward silence)*

They hear a distant drumbeat

Sarah	Oh my god that must be the procession and I've not done me hair or put me face on.
Phyllis	You've time yet. Anyway you don't want to be putting too much face on for a funeral Sarah.
Sarah	It's business Phyllis, you have to look your best don't you? *(exits)*

Knowing looks exchanged. Music of procession takes over.

Scene 2

On the Corpse Road

Up over the hill comes the procession, the Musicians, then six men carrying a coffin with **Frank Dobson**, *the funeral director, in the lead followed by a group of mourners -* **Irene Ottershaw**, *the widow, aged 65,* **Arthur Ottershaw** *(her son) (In the original production this part was created by and written for an actor with learning difficulties. The author recognizes that this may not be possible or appropriate in every production)* **Jenny Coulson** *(her daughter)* **Edna and Lucy** *(Irene's Sisters)* **Shirley Skellbrooke** *(a hanger on) and others.*

Chorus

Ruth	Here's another yarn on the horizon
Eileen	With threads that run much further back in time
May	While Sarah goes to put her face on
Margaret	Consider how our brief lives intertwine
Joan	How even over generations Familiar patterns reappear
Ruth	Dyed in the wool emotions
All 4	All human beings share.

Charlie	We can't be expected to go on much farther without another fag break Mr Dobson – it's not raight. We can't gerrus breath.
Dobson	Well … we'll put him down there for five minutes but then we must press on. We've to have the departed safely stowed in the old Dead House near Blades and be down at Mrs Harker's guest house for six.
Bob	And we mustn't disappoint Mrs Harker eh boys? *(suppressed laughter)*
Dobson	What did you say Bob?
Bob	I said we want to be there before it gets darker, Mr Dobson.
Dobson	Exactly Bob. Yes. Ladies and gentlemen, we shall just take another short rest for the sake of the bearers. As per Mr Ottershaw's instructions the band will once again play Goodnight Irene. *(Groans from mourners)*

The band strike up very gently, Goodnight Irene. Shirley starts wailing.

Shirley	Do you know Irene, it fair breaks my heart to hear that song. The number of times he sang it for you.
Irene Ottershaw (the widow)	Usually when he'd had too much. Thank you lads. That's enough. *(The band stops)*
Edna	There's no denying he liked a drink –
Lucy	All the old lead miners did, for all the Methodism and teetotaling and that.
Irene	He was always church not chapel.

Lucy	I know but, you know what I mean. They worked hard, long shifts, dust and dirt, lead miner's lung – working up a right thirst. Then they'd all get paid in a lump. No wonder they got a taste for it.
Irene	Don't make excuses for him Lucy. He wasn't in the mines that long.
Edna	No. Well he never went back did he? After the accident. After ... Never went back.
Irene	Nor he never went forward neither.
Shirley	*(crying)* waaahhh!
Irene	Oh will you give it a rest Shirley. Who invited her? Arthur are you doing what I think you're doing?
Arthur	*(zipping up)* I had to Mam, I couldn't wait any longer.
Lucy	It's so easy for men isn't it?
Irene	How much further is it from here? I've just about had enough of this now.

They wander away from the coffin. The smoking pallbearers wander back to the coffin

Charlie	Can't beat fresh air can you? *(he takes a drag)* I still don't reckon we're being paid enough for this. That last pull near killed me off and we've half a day again at least tomorrow.
Ian	I don't mind. It's traditional is this. The Corpse Way. It's keeping it alive and all that. That's what old Dan wanted.

13

Bill	Traditional? Nobody's done it for three hundred and fifty years. Not since they built the church in Muker and started burying 'em there and when they did do it, it were a wicker coffin not pine. This is just a bloody daft charade if you ask me.
Ian	I don't know, I reckon you feel like ... like you know, like you're part of something. Like you're doing summat that hundreds of men have done before you. Something really ancient and basic.
Don	Like snogging Shirley Skellbrooke behind the Village Hall on a Saturday night.
Bob	Hundreds of men have done that before.
Jim	Bloody hell! Have they? She told me I was the first.
Bill	If I can just finish my point. All this harking back to the past doesn't do anybody in the Dale any good. This is the twentieth century. We've got to be looking forward not back. Better roads. Electricity. There's plenty of places up here still haven't got it. We want more tractors and televisions and industry. We've all seen it now. The future! Before the war things had hardly changed round here for centuries, but there's no going back now.
Ian	A lot of people like the old ways. They're going to make it a National Park to preserve it.
Bill	Give me strength! National bloody Park! Do you want to live in a museum and have gormless buggers from Leeds and London queuing up to watch you cut the meadows by "traditional" methods, like a performing monkey?
Jim	Monkeys can't cut grass.

Bill	No, but they can obviously carry a coffin up an old footpath for no apparent reason.
Jim	Eh?
Jenny	Can we be getting on Mr Dobson? Mi mum's getting a bit tired.
Arthur	And a bit tetchy.
Dobson	Of course. Come on lads, let's shoulder arms – Mrs Ottershaw's anxious to be getting on. Remember it's free beer and bed and board for you all this evening. *(They pick up the coffin again)*
Ian	That's one part of the tradition you'll not turn your nose up at, Bill.
Bill	No, fair do's. That's generous of the family.
Dobson	Lead on then. *(They start to walk)*
Jim *(to Don)*	Here, 'ave you really snogged Shirley Skellbrooke?
Pallbearers *(in unison)*	Yes!

MUSIC

The procession moves on. This may be created by scenery moving rather than the procession. The Dead House and trestle approach. A couple of hikers go by in the opposite direction and stop to watch.

15

Scene 3

The Dead House

Dobson   Right, rest the coffin here lads please - Mrs Coulson - Mr Ottershaw's daughter would like to say a few words.

Jenny Coulson We're leaving the coffin here in this old barn overnight. I know you can't all join us for the last part tomorrow so on behalf of my mother and our Arthur I'd like to thank you all for accompanying us on this walk. You all know that my dad hankered after old traditions, history and old folk tales and the like. We used to say he was stuck in the past. He wasn't that old but he was born in a different world - candles and carriages, Queen Victoria. He'd read up on a lot of things and that's where he got this idea for his own funeral I suppose. Dad, if you're watching us now, I hope this is what you wanted. And thanks to the Simon Stone Sextet (all five of you) for the musical accompaniment. They'll be playing in the more accustomed setting of Harker's barn this evening after supper. Mother and Arthur and I would be pleased if you could all stay for supper. *(She gets out a pair of clogs)* We're going to leave these on the lid – to weigh it down, so he can't make a run for it – some of you might not know that in his youth my dad did a bit of clog dancing. These were his clogs. Mam?

Mrs Ottershaw comes forward and lays them on the coffin.

16

Irene	Right, next stop Harker's Hotel – I could murder a cup of tea.
Arthur	I want to say something *(he steps up to coffin)* ... Goodnight Dad. Sleep tight. Hope the bugs don't bite. Say hello to our Kit from me.
Jenny	Come on now Arthur.

They set off downhill

Dobson	Right lads, have you decided who's stopping up here?
Don	You what??
Dobson	Well somebody's got to keep an eye on the coffin overnight.
Bill	What for? He's not going anywhere.
Jim	Don't look at me – I'm not stopping out here with a dead body while you all go off and get dead drunk.
Bob	Well I think it's your responsibility Mr Dobson – as funeral director.
Dobson	Don't be ridiculous. I've got far too much to sort out down below. *(general snigger)* Well perhaps we can leave it for now, but somebody'll have to come back later.
Charlie	We should draw lots, shortest straw and that.
Dobson	All right – but get a move on.

They do so over the coffin

Mrs Walker	What are they doing darling? Isn't it marvellous?

Mr Walker	I expect it's some sort of folk ritual dear. That's what we've lost in the city. These people up here are still in touch with their roots.
Jim	Oh bloody hell! *(General laughter. They march off)*
Mrs Walker	Marvellous. *(She wanders back to take a look)*

Spooky MUSIC

Mrs Walker	Do you suppose there really is a body in there? I should have thought that was illegal or something. *(Music rises and she looks around, reads)* Daniel Ottershaw 1885 to 1953. Johnny, Johnny, wait for me darling. There's a strange feeling in that place. Have a look at the map. What's it called?
Mr Walker	I already did. Dead House. Come on, best foot forward.

3 or 4 of the chorus appear.

Ruth	Daniel Ottershaw of this parish Passed this way but once.
Eileen	And now he's vanished Into darkness and is gone.
Ruth	But where we tread we can't help leaving footprints
May	And paths for other folk who come along.

Scene 4

The Wake 1

Cut to the party. Band is playing Cheek to Cheek. Some people are dancing. Kit is wandering around but being ignored. Dobson is trying to dance with Sarah. He whispers something in her ear.

Sarah   No Frank, not tonight. It's not appropriate. I think you've had too much to drink already. Anyway, I've had to put Christopher's bed in my room to make space.

Edna   *(moving through dancers with drink)* Here you are Irene. Are you sure you wouldn't rather go home love. I'm sure that nice Mr Dobson would drive you in his car. Only some of the young uns'll be getting out of hand I shouldn't wonder, with all this free drink and it doesn't seem right with Dan not even cold ... Hardly proper for a funeral.

Irene   It's what he wanted – a party. He didn't want people being gloomy. That's rich coming from him.

Lucy   Look at your Jennifer. Have you seen them shoes she's changed into? Stilettos, I ask you. They're all the rage apparently.

Irene   Not in Reeth they're not. Where's our Arthur?

Lucy   He's alright. He's over there.

Arthur	*(He is sitting with Kit)* I had a brother called Kit you know. Like you.
Kit	Did you?
Arthur	He was my dad's favourite. He died though, a long time ago.
Irene	*(calling)* Arthur, come and sit by me for a bit.
Lucy	Well I was thinking of going to bed but I'll not get much sleep with this racket going on.
Edna	Do you know, I never knew they had so many rooms in this place and they've put camp beds up in the barn for the chaps. Mr Dobson borrowed 'em off the camp, army issue, she's made 'em ever so nice.
Irene	Edna love.
Edna	Yes.
Irene	Can we just be quiet for a bit?
Edna	Yes, I'm sorry.
Kit	Oh Mum ... I nearly forgot. Mrs Hargreaves says where's the sweet sherry, we've nearly run out.
Dobson	Hello Christopher.
Kit	*(pause)* Hello.
Sarah	That's funny, I'm sure we had enough. I might have another bottle in the cellar. I'll go and have a look.
Dobson	So Christopher – you've had to move in with your mother tonight. That must feel funny for a lad of your age.

20

Kit	What do you mean?
Dobson	Well you're a bit grown up to be sleeping with your mam. Don't worry, I won't tell any of the other lads. Hey! I'll tell you what, I might have a job for you. What do you say?
Kit	What job?
Dobson	Could be some pocket money in it for you. You're not scared of the dark are you?
Kit	No, course not.
Dobson	On second thoughts no. I don't suppose your mother would allow it.
Kit	She lets me do lots of things.
Dobson	Well, if you're sure she won't mind. It would help me out.
Kit	What is it?
Dobson	You know Mr Ottershaw's coffin that we've left up at the Dead House near Blades.
Kit	Yes.
Dobson	Well it needs guarding overnight. Not that anything might happen but, you know, as a mark of respect. Like soldiers guarding King George's coffin last year, remember?
Kit	My dad's a soldier.
Dobson	I know. That's why I thought maybes you'd be up for it. You see I need somebody I can trust. I'd get Jim Foggit to do it but he's useless. There's five bob in it for you.

	What do you reckon? *(Kit hesitates)* Oh I see. You're probably a bit frightened. A coffin, the Dead House, a bit spooky eh? – never mind.
Kit	No, I'll do it.
Dobson	Good lad. Right, you get your coat on and take a bottle of pop and packet of crisps from behind the bar. Tell 'em Mr Dobson said to put it on the slate.
Kit	I should tell me mam where I'm going.
Dobson	I'll sort it all out with her. She's busy now and you don't want her stopping you, do you? Here's half a crown now and you'll get the other one first thing tomorrow morning if you stay on guard *all* night. Get yourself off! I don't want to leave old Mr Ottershaw without his guard of honour a moment longer than necessary.

He salutes. Kit exits.

Dobson	Jim, never mind about having to go back to the Dead House. I'll do it. *(moving off)*
Jim	Thanks very much Mr Dobson.
Bill	What's got into him?
Charlie	That's an unexpected streak of generosity.
Jim	Well here's to old Dan Ottershaw's generosity.
Bob	What kinda beer is that you're drinking Jimmy? It's a funny colour.
Jim	I don't know. Who cares, it's free. This is me third pint.
Bob	Give it here *(tasting it – spits out)*.

Jim   What?

Bob   It's sweet sherry!

Shirley moves across followed by Don

Don   And did you hear how Norman Longstaff died – him as lived across from Grinton Church? Well him and his wife used to make love every Sunday morning to the sound of the church bells. Religiously. It was up with the ding and down with the dong. Up with the ding and down with the dong ... And if that fire engine hadn't gone past he'd be alive today.

Shirley That's so tasteless Don Barker *(she exits)*.

Don   No, no, it's a joke!! Shirley! Shirley!

(He follows her off. Jim winks at the others, goes after them)

MUSIC – *contemporary fifties fades into a drone.*

Scene 5

On the moor

Chorus

Ruth   A midsummer night on Melbecks Moor
            Might make many people shiver

Eileen   But balaclava'd brave Kit Harker
            Sets off from his Mum's back door

Phyllis   And takes a path up by a little river

Margaret Clutching a torch his dead dad gave him
            When National Service took him off to war.

MUSIC

We see Kit's evening journey – sheep, drystone walls, squeezes, trees. He disappears over the hill. The Dead House is reformed/revealed. By the coffin, he marches up and down like a soldier, gets bored and falls asleep. Some of the chorus are there.

Ruth lifts Kit up and places him by the coffin stone

Ruth   And now we'll knit these stories in together

Eileen   Call it fate or just blind circumstance

May   We'll make a stitch in time. It's now or never

ALL   Come out Dan Ottershaw for one last dance

24

MUSIC

Coffin opens and Dan comes out. He has two pennies on his eyes.

Dan	By heck this is not what I was expecting. I allus was one for saying Yorkshire were God's own country but ah never thought 'eaven'd turn aht to be spittin' image of upper Swaledale, right down to the drystone walls ... *(noticing the chorus)* and t'miserable looking locals. Unless I'm in the other place – aye that's more likely all things considered –
May	Come out Dan Ottershaw for one last chance
Margaret	Put on your clogs for one last dance.
Dan	Is this 'eaven?
Ruth	Not yet Dan
Eileen	You're not quite there
May	You've got to let go of what's holding you here.
Dan	Ah'd y'mean? Ahm dead aren't ah? Ah seem to remember that. Where am I?
Ruth	Dead
Eileen	But not departed
May	A sort of halfway house
Ruth	Until you're laid in consecrated You've got one last chance
Dan	Chance to do what?

Ruth	Till dawn tomorrow when They come to take you down Your spirit's free to wander All around
Eileen	To look back on your life And loves and longing To say a last goodbye Before the morning
May	Not everyone gets the chance you're getting
Margaret	They pass on to the other side regretting.
Dan	How'd you mean?
Ruth	Look down there at that lad – do you recognize him?
Dan	Kit, is it Kit?
Chorus	Yes, but not your Kit
Eileen	Another Kit – another time
Dan	What's he to do with me then?
Ruth	He's your burden and your penance. You carried one Kit on your back for more than half your life and now you must carry another through one last night
Eileen	You're bound together
Ruth	Your stories intertwine
May	One thing always finds another
Margaret	Somewhere down the line

26

He picks up the sleeping Kit and sets him piggy-back on his back

Dan   Till dawn? *(they nod)*

All   Till dawn

MUSIC Mr Sandman send me a dream (This is a kind of production number with the band on stage and the chorus setting up a landscape that Dan and Kit are moving through)

Simon Stone Thank you very much. The band are going to take
                 a short break now. We'll be back with some old
                 favourites and requests in about 15 minutes, thank you

Interval

Scene 6

Wake 2

We hear distant music from the Sextet. Sarah sits outside with Irene, Edna, Lucy and others.

Sarah   The thing is, I don't know what to do for the best Irene. I mean what future is there for us here in the Dale? Harry was always saying we'll give it one more year, one more year. And finally it turned out he didn't have one more year. He always had the fantasy of going to exotic foreign places.

Edna   I went to Bedale once. I didn't like it.

Irene   Edna, will you give it a rest.

Edna   Oh yes sorry. Sorry Sarah love.

Irene   You were saying about Harry wanting to go abroad.

Sarah   Aye Australia. My brother's out there already you see. Got a lovely house, 10 minutes from a beach. He wants us to go out there. Me and Kit.

Lucy   He's an electrician isn't he, your Stan?

Sarah   Learned it in the navy during the war. You see Harry felt he missed out on all that by staying at home on the farm. Felt a bit guilty.

28

Joan	Somebody had to else we should've all starved. We had to dig for victory, remember?
Edna	There was land girls.
Irene	Edna!
Sarah	That's why he joined the Territorials after the war. He felt he hadn't really done his bit. Then this business in Korea starts and he gets called up and in a matter of weeks he's gone. Just like that.
Irene	And you've heard no more. We all thought, you know, when them prisoners came home, that maybe, you know …
Sarah	When I get back, he says. When I get back, we'll make proper plans. We'll do up the house, convert the barn into accommodation and then we'll sell up and go to live near your Stan in Adelaide. You wait he says, next year. Next year. Next year we'll be looking at kangaroos and koalas, and merinos instead of Swaledales, kookaburras instead of curlews. Kit loves it when he talks like that. Loved it.
Irene	He's a bit of a dreamer your Kit, like his dad.
Edna	Irene had a son called Kit. Did you know that Sarah?
Sarah	He'd say to Kit – 'What do you get when you cross a kangaroo and a Swaledale sheep?' Then they'd both wait a few seconds grinning at each other and then they'd both go 'A visit from the Ministry of Agriculture'
Irene	You both must miss him.
Edna	Shouldn't it be "a woolly jumper"?

Lucy	It must be hard to keep this place going on your own. Still you're young enough yet, isn't she, Irene? I expect you could make a good catch with this place as your bait. I mean, there's one or two eligible bachelors around tonight for instance.
Edna	Frank Dobson for one.
Lucy	Bees round the honey pot.
Irene	Take no notice of them Sarah. Some people have got about as much tact as a bull in a china shop.
Edna	I'm only saying.
Irene	Well don't!
Sarah	It's alright Irene. She's only saying what everybody's thinking.
Irene	I'll tell you this for what it's worth. When I married Dan Ottershaw he was the only one I'd ever been with. He's the only man I ever ... you know. Ever.
Edna/Lucy	Irene!
Irene	The point is there wasn't a lot of choice. You only ever met a few lads of your own age.
Edna	If you were lucky.
Irene	But you've more options nowadays. Frank Dobson might seem like a big fish round here but this is a small pond. A backwater. You could do better.
Sarah	But on me own could be even worse. I don't know, Irene. What must you think of me going on about my problems when you've just lost your Dan. Can I get you anything? Shall I tell the band to finish so you can get to bed?

Irene	No I'm alright. And don't you worry Sarah. Dan Ottershaw might have died last week but I lost him a long time ago. And as it doesn't look like there'll ever be a wake for your Harry now, I don't mind you sharing mine. Come on, let's go in. It's turning cold, *(they exit)* Where is your Kit anyway?

MUSIC

Scene 7

The Toll Bridge

Cut to Dan hurrying along with the sleeping Kit on his back.
Kit wakes up.

Kit	Where am I?
Dan	Just what I was thinking. This is a rum do and no mistake. I've walked and worked up and down the dales all me life and all of a sudden I've lost me sense of direction. Where am I? How long have I been walking?
Kit	I'm dreaming.
Dan	Happen we both are.
Tollman	Stop there. If you want to cross, there's the toll to pay - tuppence per person per trip -
Dan	What's on the other side?
Tollman	It depends where you're coming from.
Dan	You what?
Tollman	It depends where you're coming from. If you're coming from Leyburn it's Middleham. If you're coming from Middleham it's Leyburn. Do you see my point? Either way it's tuppence per person.

Dan	Well, where am I coming from?
Tollman	If you don't know that you're going to have a job getting to where you're going.
Dan	Where am I going?
Tollman	Oh I see. You want spiritual guidance. Well, to my way of thinking in many ways, life is rather like a bridge.
Dan	You would say that, you're a bridge keeper.
Tollman	Each passing moment we cross the bridge of the present from the past into the future. At each crossing we pay a toll in pain or pleasure until we're all spent up. And then there is only one more river to cross and that's the river of Jordan.
Dan	Jordan? I thought this was the Ure. Now I am completely lost.
Tollman	If you're lost, I often think it's best to go back to where you started from.
Dan	Alright, which way's that?
Tollman	Looking at you I'd say about 70 years in that direction.
Dan	Right here's tuppence.
Tollman	What about the lad?
Dan	What lad?
Tollman	On your back.
Dan	I'll carry him across. His feet won't touch the bridge.
Tollman	Tuppence per person per trip.

Dan	If I carry him it's only like one.
Tollman	Tuppence per person.
Dan	That's all I've got.
Tollman	I'll take that torch.
Kit	No that's my dad's. I can't.
Dan	How much for baggage?
Tollman	Baggage? *(suspiciously)* ... No charge.
Dan	Right. *(He moves off, puts Kit down)* Get yourself in this sack.

Kit climbs in

Kit	You'd best leave me behind.
Dan	No. No. I can't do that! Not this time.

(Dan lifts bag, starts to cross the bridge)

Dan	One please.
Tollman	One way or return?

Scene 8

Wake 3

MUSIC and back to party. Simon Stone Sextet are playing/singing 'Travelling Light' (Cliff Richard).
Dobson is playing Wallops with some of the men in the street.
Sarah goes past with a tray of empties, calls out.

Ian   I suppose you call this another bit of pointless tradition then, Bill.

Bill   I don't say it's all daft. All I'm saying is times change. Right now most people round here are born and bred.

Ian   Hefted.

Bill   But in a few years they'll be more incomers than locals, then after a while the incomers <u>are</u> the locals. Celts, Saxons, Vikings, Normans. Miners, farmers, holidaymakers. The tides come and go.

Ian   It's the pace of change that matters though. You don't want to throw the baby out with the bath water.

Dobson   *(singing along)* I just can't wait to be with my baby tonight.

Sarah   Frank have you seen Kit anywhere? It's time he was in bed.

Dobson	He'll be alright, you worry too much about that lad. You've got to let him grow up a bit you know.
Sarah	I know, I molly-coddle him a bit ...
Dobson	Well, I was going to tell you. I've ...
Sarah	Only he's acting strange at the moment. I don't like to leave him alone for too long.
Dobson	Oh.
Sarah	What were you going to say?
Dobson	What?
Sarah	You were going to tell me something. About Kit.
Dobson	Yes. Er ... Does he like cricket?
Sarah	Loves it. Thinks he's going to be Fred Trueman. His dad allus used to say one day he'd take him to a county match.
Dobson	I'll do better than that. I'll take him to a test match at Headingley this summer. It's the Aussies. I'm a member, you know.
Sarah	Oh Frank, would you really? He'd love that. He's mad on Australia.
Ruth	Sarah where do you want these plates? Have we to take them back down to the village hall kitchen?
Sarah	I'm coming. *(She smiles back at Frank)*
Bob	I reckon you're in there if you play your cards right, Mr Dobson.

Dobson	She's not a bad looking woman is she? Just a bit down on her luck. I reckon I could give her a bit of a leg up.
Bob	*(sotto voce)* More like legover.
Dobson	I mean this place, if it were managed properly, could be a little gold mine - holidaymakers, ramblers, American tourists. That's a rich seam to be worked in the future, that is. I mean look at the view. There's people in London would pay good money for that.
Charlie	You're joking aren't you. Why would any bugger want to come on holiday out here. There's chuff all to do.
Dobson	Exactly. They'll come to get away from it all. Do you know how many people died last year from the smog? - 4,000 they reckon. *(Charlie puts out his fag)*
Bob	So you and Sarah Harker are an item then are you?
Dobson	Well nothing definite as yet. Harry's only been dead a year.
Bob	Missing presumed dead.
Dobson	Exactly – we are not rushing into anything. No formal announcement as yet. Sarah wants to wait.
Bill	Sounds like you've got it all mapped out though.
Dobson	Well, you can't afford to let the grass grow under your feet.
Bill	Not if you want to get your feet under the table.
Bob	Good shot

Shirley walks by followed by Don and Jim.

Jim	Can I get you another Babycham Shirley?

Shirley	Ooh go on then but then I really am going to bed.
Don	But Shirley the night is young.
Shirley	Yes but you're not, Don Barker.

She exits

Jim	Goodnight then Don.

He exits following Shirley

Charlie	Unlucky!

MUSIC *from band comes up louder again.*

"Soon I'm gonna see the love light in her eyes
I'm a hoot and a holler away from Paradise... etc"

Scene 9

Dan's mother

Music moves into droning note as Dan and Kit arrive at Dan's birthplace where a woman is holding a baby.

Mother   My baby. My little Daniel in his den.

Dan   I was born here – Gunnerside.

Kit   It looks really old-fashioned.

Dan   What do you expect, it's a lifetime ago. My dad was a lead miner. We didn't have much. Look, that's my mother, she's looking tired, looking after me. You never think about it when you're young, how much your parents struggled. Look, she's folding up the washing. She'll go and look out now to see my father coming home from the Old Gang.

Kit   The what?

Dan   The mine – they walked miles in his day above the ground and crawled miles below. In the Stang, when I worked there as a boy, a tallow candle'd burn right out before you reached the workings. The mines were still busy then. Look it's winter. Snow's up. She's put me by the fire. She was allus singing, my mother, one song or another - old folk songs, music hall, popular songs, all sorts. Does your mother sing to you?

39

Kit	I suppose. I don't know. I don't pay much notice. 'Don't sit under the apple tree with anyone else but me'. Is that one?
Dan	That's it. Don't forget them songs Kit. They're your mother's gift. When she's long gone you'll still be able to hear her sing those songs.
Mother:	*(sings)* Fourpence a day The ore is waiting in the tubs the snows upon the fell Canny folk are sleeping yet but lead is reet to sell Come me little washer lad come let's away We're bound down to slavery for fourpence a day *(Dan tearfully joins in).* Me mother gets me up at six with tears upon her cheek She packs me pack upon me back which has to last a week It often breaks her great big heart when she to me doth say I never thought you'd work mi'lad for fourpence a day.

The chorus of watching women join in

Chorus	Fourpence a day, fourpence a day I never thought you'd work mi'lad for fourpence a day.
Kit	Am I dreaming this?
Dan	Good question. Am I dreaming you or are you dreaming me?
Kit	In Australia the Aborigines have a thing called dreamtime.
Dan	Well happen we're a couple of aboriginal dalesmen.

MUSIC

40

Scene 10

Wake 4

Back at party a group of girls are doing a Beverley/Andrews Sisters number.
"Don't sit under the apple tree with anyone else but me"
There is applause. A group is talking together

Phyllis   Who asked for that one? That's a bit pointed isn't it.
She'd have a dickey fit if he did come marching home
now.

Betty   Who?

Jane   Harry, of course.

Phyllis   That would upset the apple cart.

Sarah   *(enters)* Has anyone seen Kit? I'm getting a bit worried
now.

Jane   He's not hidden himself in the log box again has he?

Phyllis   Well he can't be far away can he?

MUSIC

41

Scene 11

Dan moves on

Cut to Kit being carried by Dan.
Landscape rushes by. Names of old mines flash by.

Kit   Where are we now?

Dan   Further on. Much further on. We've left the lead mines behind, them days are behind us now. They can't make 'em economic no more. Cheaper lead elsewhere, Australia for one. I worked in the mines as a lad, like me dad and grandad before but they were all but played out. I ended up farming and odd jobbing. Carried me wallet, as they say, up and over and worked on Lord Bolton's estate. I was young and strong then, I used to clog dance at fairs and market days. I had a bit of a name for it.

Kit   You used to dance?

Dan   You young'uns never think old folk ever did owt.

(he demonstrates dancing)

Mother   You're good at that our Dan. You should go up to Leyburn to that Tournament of Song and do your act. There's choirs and musicians and stalls. You might win a prize.

Kit   Did you?

42

Dan	Oh I went there all right and I did win a prize, but not for clog dancing.

Three choirs enter with signs Hawes, Richmond, Leyburn
3 young girls run past Dan. One of them drops a bag and goes back for it

Yng Lucy	Hurry up Irene.
Dan	There was these three lasses in one choir, sisters. One of 'em kept looking at me and I kept looking at her.
Yng Edna	Irene are you coming to choir or not? I'll tell mother!

Song Tournament starts up again and battle rises to cacophony

Judge	Thank you ladies and gentlemen. The judges will now retire to consider their verdict.
Yng Lucy	What's your name?
Dan	Dan Ottershaw. What's yours?
Yng Lucy	Lucy Rawcroft.
Yng Edna	Edna Rawcroft and this is our Irene *(They giggle)*
Dan	I was better looking then.
Yng Lucy	Show us your clog dancing then.
Yng Edna	Go on if you're so good.
Yng Lucy	Who did you think was the best choir?
Yng Edna	You work for Lord Bolton don't you?
Yng Lucy	Where did you get that fancy suit?
Dan	I said to her, the quiet one, 'Are you walking out with anyone?'

43

Yng Irene	No.
Yng Edna	Irene!
Dan	Will you walk out with me?
Yng Irene	Yes.
Yng Edna	Irene!
Yng Lucy	Have you got any brothers?
Dan	I married her the following year. We lived in a cottage on the estate. We were hard up but happy then. First we had our Kit, then our Jennifer then Arthur.
Kit	Kit? That's my name.
Dan	Aye and he was about your age when we lost him.
Kit	Lost him?

Jump in time – young girl Irene re-costumes and turns into wife and mother Irene, she treats Kit as her Kit. A young Jenny and a young Arthur are also there.

Yng Irene	So you're going to take him up there with you. Jenny pass me that bag.
Dan	He wants to go – like father, like son. They allus say Swaledale lads are born with a pick in their mouths.
Yng Irene	It's bad enough you going down the mines again after all these years.
Dan	Irene, it's our big chance. They've opened up again at Faggergill and they're looking for experienced men. We could make proper money. I'm going in with Jake Stubbs and Sydney Hird. We've a good bargain.

44

Yng Irene	He's barely old enough Dan. I'd rather he stayed on at school.
Dan	And how do we pay for that? I went with my dad when I was his age. You molly-coddle him too much Irene.
Yng Irene	I don't care. You said yourself them levels up there are unstable.
Dan	That's why they've never been worked out. Why there's still lead to be had.
Yng Irene	At what price?
Dan	The price is good at the moment.
Yng Irene	That's not what I meant Daniel. *(Pause)*
Y Arthur	Can I go with Kit? I want to go with Kit.
Y Irene	No Arthur. Jenny, take Arthur to play outside.
Jenny	That's not fair, I always have to look after Arthur. I want to wave Kit off.
	(sings) Goodbyee, Goodbyee,
Kit/Jenny/Arthur	Wipe the tear baby dear from your eyeee
Yng Irene	Stop that. He's not going to war. *(She dresses Kit with scarf and hat and gives him bag)* Here's your bait son. Stick close to your dad. You take care of him. If anything happens to him …

45

Scene 12

Wake 5

Cut back to party. Sarah and Dobson mid argument.

Sarah   ... If anything happens to him I'll ... The Dead House? How could you do such a thing? He might run away or something stupid. He's been acting up recently, shutting himself in cupboards, daydreaming. Always on about his dad coming back. He always has a bit of a mood when you're around.

Dobson   I was going to tell you. I gave him a little job to do, keep him occupied. It's a lovely warm midsummer night. He'll be fine. It'll do him good. I'll go up and get him later if you're that bothered. I thought it might give us a bit of privacy for a change.

Sarah   Privacy? With 20 guests in the house? In any case, he's 13 years old, Frank. What were you thinking of?

Dobson   You know very well what I'm thinking of. You can't keep me hanging on forever you know. You can't keep using Kit as an excuse to keep me at arms length. Are you going to let ...

Shirley   *(Walking through)* Look Don, Jim, I'm sure you're both very nice and I admit I have enjoyed our little conversations, but really you have to realise a modern women is looking for a bit more than a kiss me quick behind the village hall *(exits).*

46

Dobson	Are you going to let a sulky teenager stand in the way of your future, our future?
Sarah	What future's that Frank?
Dobson	Oh come on. Don't start playing hard to get now. You ought to show me a bit of gratitude. The Ottershaw family have spent a lot of money on this do and most of it's gone to you. D'you think Wilberforces would have chosen this crabby little hotel for the wake if it hadn't been for me? Your Harry let it go to pot, you've said that to me yourself. Always going to sort it out tomorrow. Well I'm not a man that likes to wait till tomorrow. You told me the bank was breathing down your neck. I had a word with Mr Clarkson over a game of golf. You said you were desperate for business else you'd have to sell up. Now you can get straight. You've me to thank for that. Once we've got this place on an even keel there'll be no stopping us.
Sarah	Us? You're going so quick you've overtaken yourself. Let's go back a step or two. I thought it was me you were interested in, not a business opportunity.
Dobson	Of course it's you.
Sarah	And you thought you'd get Kit out of the way did you? You really thought I'd be snuggling up to you while Kit slept out on the tops all night? If you thought that you don't know me at all.
Dobson	Oh come on Sarah. All this fuss because I pulled a trick on poor little Christopher. I've told you I'll go and get him. I thought you'd be glad of a chance for us to be together without him sitting between us on the sofa. Are you going to let him rule the roost forever?

You want to tell him to let his dad go and let his mum get on with the rest of her life.

Sarah	Oh you're right there Frank. His Mum has got to get on with the rest of her life and we've both got to let go of Harry, but we'll do it when we're ready. Not according to your business plan. Now get out of my way, I'm going to go and get my son.

Scene 13

Mining Accident

The Chorus create mining tunnels. Kit and Dan are seen crawling and working. This scene blurs time and space. 1950s Kit has "become" Dan's son Kit. It is part of Dan's Dreamtime Last Dance, so he is both talking to 1950s Kit or narrating events, and also talking and re-living with his son Kit and his wife Irene.

Dan	2000 years! Think of that. "When Julius Caesar was a king, Arkendale mines was a famous thing."
Kit	Julius Caesar! And we're still digging in the same place.
Dan	The more things change the more they stay the same. Down here son this way ...
Kit	I can feel a draught.
Dan	It's the old man. The old man's been here.
Kit	What old man?
Dan	Old working folk from the past, previous generations. Mebbes centuries ago. Them that been here before us. We'd best pull back till we've got more props. It could be loose – back fill.
Kit	Dad there's a whole tunnel here.
Dan	I said to him, I did, I told him to come back. Kit!

There is a collapse Kit is buried.

Dan   No. No. Kit! Can you hear me. Hold on son. I am going to get help. We'll have you out. (*He turns away out of the scene and into another*)

Yng Irene   You left! You left 'im there on his own – in the dark.

Dan   No. Yes. I have to get help. We need more hands to get him out.

Yng Irene   I'm going into him. You do what you have to do.

Dan   You'll not find him in the dark.

Yng Irene   I'll find him.

She enters the tunnels, created by the chorus, calling out for Kit.

Yng Irene: Kit! Kit! Where are you?!

Sarah   (*coming from the real world*) Kit! Kit!

Young Irene finds Kit's hand sticking out of the rubble – she takes it

Yng Irene   Don't worry son, I'm here now. Your dad'll be back soon with help. Squeeze my hand if you can hear me.

Sarah   Christopher - it's your mum love- where are you?

Yng Irene   Christopher, don't let go. No don't let go.

Sarah   Here you are. Come on Christopher wake up.

Kit climbs out as Young Irene fades away to stand with Dan. Sleepy 1950s Kit is still half in his dream. He sees both his real mum and Dan and Irene.

Dan   Irene – I don't know what to say.

Yng Irene	Don't speak to me Dan Ottershaw.
Kit	*(Speaking to dream characters)* It wasn't his fault.
Sarah	Come on Kit snap out of it. Oh you're frozen half to death.
Kit	It wasn't his fault.
Sarah	It certainly was and I've given him a piece of my mind. You will be pleased to know we'll not be seeing so much of Mr Dobson after tonight.
Kit	*(to dream Dan)* Don't blame yourself.
Sarah	I do Kit. I've been stupid, but I've come to my senses now.
Kit	Don't blame yourself Dan.
Sarah	Dan! Who are you talking about?
Kit	Mr Ottershaw.
Sarah	Eh? Come on you've been dreaming again. Let's get you home.

They set off towards home.

Kit	*(to Sarah)* I left my torch – Dad's torch.
Sarah	Hurry up.

He runs back to Dan

Dan	Listen. This is important. I lost my lad, but I wouldn't let him go. I carried him on my back for the rest of my life. I made it hard for my other two kids. I made it miserable for my wife. I just stopped see, I wouldn't cross the next bridge. I kept going over and over the

same ground – what if, if only. I wanted time to go backwards - for things to be back where they were. It won't – they can't. So I let my life go by instead of travelling into it, but I am going across that final bridge now. *(He climbs back into the coffin)* Don't forget the past, but don't let it stop you from moving on. *(He lies down.)*

Kit   Dan

Dan   Yes

Kit picks up the torch, looks at it, then puts it in the coffin. Dan understands the meaning of the gesture. They shake hands. Kit closes the coffin then runs after his mum.

Sarah   Have you found it?

Kit   No

Sarah   Oh dear.

Kit   It's alright, it doesn't matter.

Sarah   Are you sure? Well if we don't find it in the morning I'll get you a new one. And I'll tell you another thing we'll do tomorrow. We're going to write to the Australian Embassy and to your Uncle Stan in Adelaide.

Scene 14

The Churchyard at Grinton

A single bell tolls.

MUSIC – Lyke Wake dirge

> *Hark from the toll the dolesome sound,*
> *Thine ears attend the cry.*
> *Ye living men come view the ground*
> *Where ye must surely lie.*

The procession reforms and the coffin is brought to Grinton churchyard.

Chorus   In Grinton church, cathedral of the dales
              They lay Dan Ottershaw to rest
              They say that in such places an atmosphere prevails
              A sense of history, of time compressed
              The ancient and the recent and what hasn't happened yet.

The mourners are standing around the coffin.
Brollies are used to make a mound.

Vicar   Ashes to ashes,
              Dust to dust
              In sure and certain hope of a resurrection to a life hereafter.

              Family place flowers

53

Charlie	It's times like this you just want to lie down and die.
Bob	I know, I've got a splitting headache.
Jim	And a mouth like the bottom of a budgie's cage.
Ian	Show a bit of respect lads.
Bill	I just want to put me feet in a bowl of hot water.
Don	Psst, psst ... Shirley!
Shirley	What?
Don	What are you doing after?
Bob	He never gives up does he?
Shirley	Frank's ... Mr Dobson's going to pick me up in his car and take me home actually.
Don & Jim	Bloody hell!

The 1950s scene begins to dissolve away slowly like ghosts hanging around the gravestones as an Australian woman and her two children appear. They are clearly from the present (2005) They are looking at gravestones. They cannot see the 1950s characters.

Alex	This is a bit freaky mum. Can't we go and get an ice cream?
Kate	*(to a chorus member who has become **Older Susan** and is doing flowers)* Excuse me, do you know where we might find the grave of a Daniel Ottershaw. He died in the 1950s.
Older Susan	Well, I am not sure but Mrs Little might know. Is he a relative?

Kate	No but my father came from here – Christopher Harker.
Older Susan	I remember Kit Harker, we were at school together. I'm Susan Robinson, Hargreaves as was. Him and his mother went to Australia. And you're his daughter?
Kate	That's right.
Older Susan	Well I never!
Tom	Here it is Mum, I think this is the one – *(reads)* 'Daniel Ottershaw 1885 – 1953 and also his wife Irene 1887 – 1964. Reunited'. Is this it?
Kate	Yes, put the flowers on it Alex.
Alex	Is this one of our relatives Mum?
Kate	It's somebody Grandad Kit used to talk about a lot. I promised him we'd put some flowers on the grave.
Tom	He used to go on and on about the Dales and its history. If he liked it so much why did he leave?
Alex	We would never have been born if he hadn't stupid.
Kate	Excuse me Mrs Robinson, er Susan. Can you tell us how to get onto the Corpse Way?
Older Susan	Oooh, do you have a car?

MUSIC

Scene 15

Australia relinquishes the Ashes

Chorus

Ruth   From the Peat Gate Head and Barney Beck, among the ruins of the mines, it's quite a climb to Barfside and beyond

Eileen   From where we're standing now, in so called modern times It sometimes takes some thought to see the human bond

May   That ties us to the people of the past

Margaret And weaves our many stories into one

Joan   Yet here we are again at last

All   Another rite of passage and another song.

Tom   It's really cold up here Mum.

Alex   Is this really Summer?

Kate   Come on it won't take long.

Tom   Shall I do it now?

Kate   Why not.

(She puts on music: 'Time of your life' by Green Day, from ghetto blaster whilst he takes an urn out of his rucksack)

Kate   Go on.

He/they scatter ashes to the wind.

Kate	Goodbye Dad.
Alex & Tom	Goodbye Grandad Kit.
Kate	Now then, what was Grandad Kit's surname? My name before I married your dad?
Tom	Harker.
Kate	See that hillside over there?
Alex & Tom	Yeah.
Kate	Do you know what it's called – Harkerside.
Tom	Wow!
Alex	How cool is that!
Tom	Does it belong to us?
Kate	No, but in a way you belong to it.

Pause as they stare out

Alex	Can we have an ice cream now?

CHORUS et al take up the song from ghetto blaster 'Time of your Life' by Green Day'.